"Zee 'ee Dreckly"

by

JOHN GERMON

First published in Great Britain in 1995

Orchard Publications
2 Orchard Close, Chudleigh, Newton Abbot, Devon. TQ13 0LR
Telephone: (01626) 852714

ISBN. 1 898964 16 5

Designed, Typeset and Printed for Orchard Publications by
SWIFT PRINT
2, High Street, Dawlish, S. Devon. EX7 9HP

VORWARD

In Devon there are many variations of dialect and words, North, South, East, all have their variations. Equally throughout Devon, Cornwall, Somerset and Dorset, borders are no barrier to dialect and that is why you will often hear very similar words in each county, of course Devon is the correct one, we have just lent them to the rest!

I am often asked how Devon dialect is written, the simple answer is "You spell it how you say it", and that is why the written dialect varies, depending on which part of Devon you come from.

A good example of this was a word I mentioned on B.B.C. Radio Devon – 'Grutus' – the part of the plough that turns the furrow. Having mentioned this word a huge amount of correspondence was received and variations were as follows: Gridus, Grawdus, Mould Board, Groot Rest. On checking this out it has been suggested that the original word was in fact 'Groot Rest', Groot (untilled soil) being put to Rest (turned), and the rest of the words are a corruption of this. Another example is for the Foxglove, you can have a choice of: Floppy Doc, Cow Flop (the two most common), followed by Proud Ladies, Mountain Tulips, Fairy Thimbles, and so on. So you can see there are many variations to take into account.

Pronunciation of letters in Devon dialect you will notice change, for example the letter S can become Z. F is often changed for V. O is sometimes changed for an A. The OO will often sound like U.

EXAMPLE:

Sunday	Zunday, Zinday
Summer	Zummer
Sand	Zand
Fast	Vast
Farmer	Varmer
Fish	Veesh
Fool	Vule
Stop	Stap
Proper	Praper

There are of course a lot more, but if I told you all of them you might get a bit too Edificated (Educated). So enough of this ole Rigmarole, I hope you may find this book of some use and interest, and don't be afraid to use some of the words, it will show people that you know how to talk proper.

"Cheers me boodys 'n uz'l zee 'ee DRECKLY".

John Germon

1

A Dialect Alphabet

A	Apple	*As red as a rawze (rose).*
B	Bule	*With a ring droo 'ees nawse (nose).*
C	Cow	*Vull 'o 'ees own charm.*
D	Dumplin	*Deb'm volk oo wont do 'ee no harm.*
E	Edification	*Make 'ee wise at 'th end 'o 'th day.*
F	Finniky	*Zome maid oo dawnt like rompin' 'n 'th hay.*
G	Granfer Grigg	*With 'ees bandy ole legs.*
H	Hen	*A layin' thikky eggs.*
I	Ivery whips 'n while	*Meaning' now 'n agaan (again).*
J	Junket	*Like mother maaks, 'twill never be 'th saam.*
K	Kitty Tope	*A Jenny Wren gatherin' grub.*
L	Leery	*Why not git a pasty 'n a pub.*
M	Mump Aid	*'Ee got 'th brains 'o a brick wall.*
N	Nort	*Meaning nothing at all.*
O	Osses	*Worrited be vlies.*
P	Pigs	*Layin' down 'n thicky sty's.*
Q	Quaazy	*Veelin' really unwell.*
R	Rawze	*Kin' 'ee call 't mind 'th smell.*
S	Scrumpy	*'Th West Countrymans Liquor.*
T	Teddy Caake	*'Twill maake 'ee graw thicker.*
U	Upitty	*Tempers grawin' quite large.*
V	Varmer	*'Th aid man 'n charge.*
W	Want Nap	*Place fer piskies 't squat.*
X	?	*Tiz fer zomethin', but I'm blawed if I naw what.*
Y	Yokel	*A bloke 'o 'th land.*
Z	Zummer	*When 'th countryzides grand.*

A Few Old Deb'm Sayin's

Cream on Pilchards.
New white coat over dirty clothing.

"Er'v only give 'n a squat 'n a bruise".
Clothing that hasn't been ironed very well.

"Tiz cold 'nough fer a fur lined walkin' stick".

A young lady passed a farmer wearing very tight jeans, and looking at
the maid's backside he said to his mate –
"Caw look at that! 'Tiz like a couple 'o verrits in a rat catcher's bag".

"You look like you bin put 'een with bread 'n tak out with the caake."
Meaning half baked.

"'Tiz blawin' 'nough to blaw thikky teeth off a zaw".

"'Ee's as much good as a dug with zide pockets".

"Watersweet even if tid'n lilly white".
Laundry washed but not very clean.

"H'appenny head 'n farthin' tailed".
New hat but down at heel.

"Nawze like a jug handle".
Big nose.

"Neck like a swanner duck".
Long neck.

I know you don't nose behind curtains but I expect you know someone who does. I think they call it Neighbourhood Watch. Well, you could accuse them of the following –
"There's more eyes on er than ther is in a SACK 'O TEDDIES!!

"You braake yer legs me boody, daw'nt you come rinnin' 't me".

"If you kill yer zel, I shan't spaake to 'ee agaan".

"They chillern by jumpin' up 'n down like a bag 'o flays (fleas)".

"Tiz like lookin' fer 'n apple on Dartmoor".
As in looking for a needle in a haystack.

"'Ee looks like 'ee be 'bout to hand een 'ees knife and fork".
Someone who is ill.

EPITAFS

Yer lies I, 'tiz no wonder I'm daid,
The wheel 'o the wagon went over me aid.

Yer be the remains 'o Jinny Crout,
If tid'n yer, 'tiz yer about.

Here lies the body of old Ned Gay
He died disputing the right 'o way,
He was right as it happened, as he rode along
But he lies here now, as if he was wrong.

Here I lie be 'th chancel door,
I lies here because I'm poor,
The further in, the more you pay,
But I sleep here, just as warm as they.

5

ABROAD   Broken to pieces.
"Look at 'th 'ole cloam pot 'ee've scat 'n abroad".

ACE, ISS, EES, AYS   Yes.
"Oh ace it do zute us to say uz be or else uz baint".

A-CHUCKED   Thirsty.
"Caw, I'm gwain down ole 'Red Dug' 't'wet me oozle'" *(see oozle)*

ADDLE AIDED
Someone who is said to be *'Addle Aided'* is a littleslow, backward.
(see Mump Aided).

ADDERS TOUNGE
Greater Stitchwork. Sometimes used for Deadly Nightshade.

ADDLED   Rotten. i.e. Rotten Eggs.

AGE-TRAWS
Hedge Troughs. Drainage ditches that can be found at the base of hedges.

AIMZES, AMEZES   Hames.
Part of a harness used for working horses.
"Zort out thikky Aimzes will 'ee, they'm lookin' a bit 'Raimid'?"

ANGLE TWITCH, ANGLE DUG   Earthworm.
*"I tell 'ee buye 'tiz no time avore 'th ole Angle Dugs 'o draw 'n down
proper"*.

ANKERCHER, ANKCHER   Handkerchief.

ANNIVERSARY CLAWS
Clothes that are worn on anniversary days, such as celebration of chapel,
Sunday School etc.

ANSTEEVE   Handle of a flail.
"This yer Anteeve be terrible 'Ramshackled".

ANZUM   Handsome.
"Caw 'er be 'n anzum cheal".

APPLEDRANE   Wasp.
"Will 'ee mop up thikky traade, else 'twill draw 'th ole appledranes to 'ee".

APSE   Hasp, Fasten.
"Why dawnt 'ee apse thikky door".

A-VEERED   Afraid.
"Look at 'th ole gurt gawk, 'ee be a-veered 'o a little ole appledrane".

AXWADDLER   Ash Peddler.
One who collected wood or peat ash. The ash would be sold to soap
manufacturers.

BAALIN', BAWLING Making a noise, shouting, calling.
"Will 'ee jist listen to that cheal, baalin' er eye balls out".

BACHELORS BUTTONS Burdock.

BACK 'OUSE Scullery, back kitchen.
"Mother 'ev 'ee zin me boots?, 'eys maid they'm out 'n 'th back 'ouse".

BACK-ZE-VORE Back to front.
"Yer gurt gawk, yer vest be Back-Ze-Vore".

BAINT Not.
"Uz Baint". (We are not). "Baint right". (It is not right).

BEASTINGS Colostrum. The first milk from a newly calved cow.

BELLER, BELLOW Shout.
"Did 'ee yer 'th ole vule beller, 'twas ' nough 't waake thikky daid".

BIDDLE Beetle.
This is another word that varies from area to area.
Another meaning is to enlarge.

BILLERS Cow parsley.

BIRDS EYE Seedwell.
This name is sometimes given to Red Campion.

BISHOPS WEED Ground Elder.
Sometimes you will hear it called *'Gout Weed'*.

BISSLY, BISSTLE, BISSLEY   Beastly. Dirty.

"Get rid 'o 'th Bissley ole thing will 'ee?".

BLACK AID   Tadpole.

BLACK ARMY   Fleas.

One of my fovourite sayings is:

"Us never had fleas in Devon 'till they built that Tamar Bridge".

BLADDERS   Blisters.

Jan Stewer in one of his famous books wrote that he had *"Bladders on both veet and was pummle vooted fer a fortnight"*.

BLESS VORE

This is an old word dating back to around 1750, meaning a charm or a spell.

BLIDDY WARRIORS   An old Devon name for Wall Flowers.

BLOOTH   Blossom.

"'Th ole blooth be maister vull this yer".

BLUE ASSED FLIES   Blow Flies.

As a child I can remember if you kept moving about, or could not keep still, they would say *"You'm like a Blue Assed Fly"*.

BOUGHTON CAAKES

This relates to products that have been bought rather than home made. i.e. Boughton Cakes, Boughton Cider, Boughton Bread, etc.

BRANDY BOTTLE   Yellow Water Lily.

BREAD & CHEESE Hawthorn leaves and berries.

BRIMMLES, BRIMBLES Brambles.
"You watch yer 'ands buye,they old Brimbles 'o scratch 'ee 't bits".

BROKEN MOUTHED Without teeth.
"This yer oss be terrible broken mouthed".

BUNGY Short, stout.
This actually is the nickname that some of my relatives have for me. (Don't go telling anyone).

BUYE, BIY, BUY Boy.

BUY'S LOVE Southern Wood.

CAAPER
Caper.

"Caw these yer rules be a proper ole caaper".

CALL TO MIND
Remember.

"Yer kin' 'ee call 't mind thikky fellers name?".

CHAWK
Jackdaw.

How can you tell the difference between rooks and Crows?.

"If there's more than two Crows in a field, they'm Rooks, If there's more than two Rooks in a field, they'm Crows"!!! (Dawnt 'ee naw nort?"

CHEAL
Child.

This usually relates to girls, as *Buy's be Buye's.*

CHIKKY
Cheeky.

"Chikky varment, if you ask me 'ee needs a good thraipin".

CHILLERN
Children.

"Look at they Chillern, they'm jumpin up 'n down like a bag 'o flay's". (Fleas).

CHIMLEY SWAAP
Chimney Sweep.

Before brushes came into use, people would use a vuz bush, which would be weighted and pulled down the chimney to the fire place.

CLAW HAMMER COAT   Tail Coat.

CLEDGEE   Sticky, muddy. Clay.
"Daw'nt 'ee go vallin' 'een there buye, 'tiz master cledgee".

CLOAM   Earthenware or clay.
'Cloamin' – made of clay. *'Cloam Omn'* — Cloam Oven.

COCKLEERT   Dawn.
It was suggested to me the other day, that it may be relating to when the
Cock Bird is alert. (Pass).

CORNISH COMPLIMENT
This would relate to a gift of no great value.
(This is not my personal opinion although it is used a lot in Devon).

COWFLOPS   Foxglove.
Also known as *'Floppy Docks'*.

CRADDID   Of acid disposition.
"I tell 'ee 'er be master craddid smornin'".

CRAMS   Nonsence.
"If you ask me, me boody, 'tiz nort but a parcel 'O Crams".

CRILLY GREENS   Curley Greens, Curley Kale.

CROWD, CROWDER   Violin, Violinist, Fiddler.

CRYING THE NECK
An ancient ceremony performed in the field when the harvest is complete.
A 'Neck' of straw was twisted, and kept until the next harvest. This was
believed to hold all the evil spirits of the harvest. (Corn Dollies).

CUZ   Because. (See section 'U').

DAP Slap.

"If you dawnt behave yerzel, I'll give 'ee sich a dap round yer, yer ole"
(Ear).

DAYCHIN Thatching. See *'Lousterin'*.

DEAR LILL' ZAW Dear little soul.

A term of endearment usually towards children, when applied to older
women it would convey sympathy such as *"Pawer Awl Zaw"* (Poor Old
Soul). For an old man *"Pawer Awl Begger"*, even if the person may be quite
wealthy.

DEESH Dish.

"Will 'ee ave a deesh 'o tay".

A phrase from when people used to drink tea from bowls without handles,
instead of cups or mugs.

DEESH WASHER Wagtail

DEEVE Deaf.

"Tiz no good talkin' 't 'ee, 'ee's Deeves a pawst".

13

DEW SNAIL   Slug.

"Jist git a scat 'o rain 'n 'th ole Dew Snails be all auver 'th plaace".

DIMPSEY, DIMMETT   Twilight.

Just as the sun has faded and it is starting to get dark.

"Tiz zaid to be getting Dimpsey".

DIP CHICK   Moorhen.

DOLLOP   A measure.

"I'll ave a dollop 'o craame".

DONNIKIN

This was a name given to the
earth privvy that you would
find at the bottom of gardens
or across yards.
I remember being amazed
at how small my grandfather's
newspapers used to be,
and how strange it was
storing them on a string

DRANGWAY   Narrow passage, alley.

"'Ee jist rinned up yonder drangway".

DRAYSH   Thrash.

"Git on buye, give 'n a good drayshin' wi' olly".

DRECKLY, DREKLY. Later on.

Cornwall will tell you that this is not Devonshire, it is Cornish. Devonians will tell you it is not Cornish, *'TIZ DEB'M!*

DREE-APPENCE Three halfpence.

"I kin call 't mind when teddies wuz Dree-Appence a bag".
(I can't but it sounds good).

DREXIL, DRECKSILL Threshold, doorstep.

"eb'm got time 't stop yer, yappin' I got 't git out 'n scrub 'th ole Drexil".

DRUMBLE DRANE Drone or Bumble Bee.

"Twaz ummin' just like a Drumble Drane on a Cowflop".

DUG, DOAG Dog.

Here in Ashburton the 'Red Lion Inn' was always known as *'Red Dug'.*

DUG MAPLE Sycamore.

EAR DROPS Fuchsia.

EDDY-F'CATION Education.

This is a mix between Edify and Education.

'EEN TU Into.

"'Ee id'n gwain een 't 'n proper like".

'EES He is, He's.

'Ees a gurt mump aid, 'n 'ee id'n eezel".

EEZEL Himself, His self.

"'O eys me boody, 'ees a vule to eezel".

15

ERBONS   Ribbons.

EVERY WHIPS 'N WHILE   Now and again.
"'Tiz stickin' 'ees aid 'een 'n out, every whips 'n while, like a fiddler's elbow".

EYS   Yes.
(Pronounced as Ace) Sometimes spelt *'ees.*

FAAGITS
Bundles of hedge cuttings, (Ashen Faggots) lit in celebration around Christmas time. Very old custom.

FANTY SHEENY   Absurdly fanciful.
"They Zinday (Sunday) clothes 'er ad on was master Fanty Sheeny".

FINNIKY   Fussy.
"If you ask me, that maid be far too finniky".

FITCH   Polecat, Ferret.
(Vitch) used for a Weasel sometimes.

FLIBBERTS   Small pieces.
Another term used for this is one of my favourites, *'Flibberty Skriddicks'.*

FLITTERMOUSE   Bat.
"What was that? It flittered past me aid". "Aw 'twas jist 'n ole Flittermouse".

FLUMMOXED   Confused, puzzled.
"Some 'o this yer Deb'm Mouthspaich kin' maake 'ee terrible Flummoxed".

FRAKSHUS   Upset.
"Caw 'th ole maid was terrible frakshus, 'n skritchin 'er aid off".

FRAWZY   Treat.

It used to be that people would have a *'Wazegooze 'n Frawzy'*, which meant an outing, ending up with a treat, something like *'Tay 'n Pasty'*.

FURN-TICKET

It is well known in Ashburton that if you took a maid up Dartmoor, you would always be asked *"Did 'ee taake yer 'Vurn Ticket' buye"*.

FUZ PIG   Hedgehog.

Sometimes called a *'Hedgy Boar'*, and *'Vuz Pig'*.

GALLIVANITIN   Getting around.

Someone always getting about is said to be off *'gallivanitin'*.

GAWK   Foolish.

"I tell 'ee, 'ees a gurt gawk".

GLEANIES   Guinea Fowl.

"I zeed thikky Gleanies oe'r yonder hills avore noon".

GOD'S 'O MIGHTY COW   Ladybird.

GOLDEN GLADDY   Yellow Hammer. Bird.

This one's for all you horny bird watchers.

GOO'COOS   Blue Bells.

There is nothing better than a nice walk in the summer, through 'a Blue Bell Woods'.

GOOD FER NORT   Good for nothing.

"That gurt guzzle guts be a good fer nort, 'ees as much good a dug with zide pockets".

GOOZE GOBS   Gooseberries.

"Do uz a faver maid will 'ee, go out 'n git uz some Gooze Gobs".

GRANFER GRIGG   Woodlouse.

Also sometimes known as *'Sow Pig'*, you will often find *Granfer Griggs in old moots.*

GRANNIES BONNET   Colembine.

GREY BIRD   Song Thrush.

Bit like mezel!

GRUTUS

This is a word that I mentioned on B.B.C. Radio Devon one day and received a lot of letters about.

The variations were: *Gridus, Grawdis, Grootus, Groot Rest and Mould Board.* On checking up it would appear that the original word was *Groot Rest* (untilled soil being put to rest).Turning a furrow as the word refers to the part of a plough that turns a furrow.

GROCKLE   Visitor.

This is a fairly recent word, but has become very common, so I think we have to include it. In Cornwall and in Devon you will hear visitors referred to as *"Emmets"* as well.

GUZZLE GUTS   To drink to extreme.

"Thikky cheal be nort but 'n ole Guzzle Guts".

GWAIN   Going.

"Where be gwain to me boody?". "If you'd 'ave asked me, I could ave told 'ee you was lost!"

HANKERCHER   Handkerchief.

"Coughs 'n sneezes spread diseases, kitch em in yer hankercher".
(Sometimes the 'H' is dropped - *'Ankercher'*).

HEABLE   Pitchfork.

"Yer buye take 'th ole Heable out 'n scat thikky straw about will 'ee?"

HECKAMAL, HAKAMAL, HECKYMAL   Tomtit.

HINKLIN   Inclination.

Again sometimes the 'H' is dropped making *'Inclin'*.
"I eb'm got no inklin to it maid".

HOLLERED, HOLLERIN   Shouted, shouting.

"They chillern be hollerin' like a craw (crow). Also 'Hallin' 'n Ballin'.

HOMESCREECH   Mistle Thrush.

"A boodiful bird, bit like the Mother-in-Law, daw'nt 'ee knaw"?

HOOP   Bullfinch.

HORNED RABBIT This is a poacher's name for Venison. If you got caught, you would say *"Zorry yer 'onner, I thought 'twas 'n 'Orned Rabbit"!*

HUSSEY

An item for resting pans on in an open hearth fire, usually attached to a crook.

ID'N 'EE   Is'n't he.

INDERZIDE   Underside.

INJIN'   Engine.

INNERDS   One's internal organs.
An example of how these could be used:
"'Ees master for takin' abroad 'th innerds of 'th ole injin', id'n 'ee? 'Ee loves gettin' all thikky bits out specially inderzide. Then if 'ees lucky, they all go's back again in a proper manner".

JEWSIVE
Possibly a corruption of 'Deuced', present usage seems to be related to 'Ever so large', i.e. *"'Twas a jewsive pain".*

JIDGE   Judge.
"You'm jist in time to yer 'th ole jidge give 'ees opinion".

JINGLE   A two wheeled vehicle drawn by a pony or cob.

JIST, JIS   Just.

JOLLOP   Medicine.
"'Er got one hang 'o a cough me boody, uz ad better give 'n zome jollop".

JONNICK   Pleasant, agreeable, easy to get on with. True.

JUNKET   Sweetened milk which has rennet added.

KAYPIN' COMP'MY   Keeping Company, courting.

"I was very fond 'o kaypin' comp'my wi' the missus, trouble was, when uz went out uz ended up with 'er Mother, Father, two Brothers, two Sisters! Do 'ee think they did'n trust me?"

KEE   An old 18th Century word for a cow.

KETCH VORE   To ketch up with.
"Uz'l aive to git a move on maid, if uz be gwain to Ketch Vore".

KICK HAMMER   Stammer.

KICKSHAW   Amusement, entertainment, exhibition.
"Caw last yer's Carnival wuz a proper Kickshaw".

KIT   Buzzard.

KITTLE, KIDDLE   Kettle.

Mother was always keen to tell 'ee to *"Put thikky Kittle on will 'ee buye?"*.

KITTY TOPE   Jenny Wren.

KURZMUS   Christmas.

LEERY   Empty.

A cart of hay that went up past you full and comes back empty is said to be
Leery. Also sometimes Leary, depending on ow posh you be.

LENT LILLIES, LENT ROSES   Wild Daffodils.

I heard someone the other day call them *'Daffle Down Dillies'. Gurt Gawk.*

LEWTH   Lew.

The side sheltered from wind and rain.

LINNEY, LINHAY

Place where carts, wagons, tools, etc. are kept. A favourite past time was
having to lime wash the Linhay.

LONG CRIPPLE   Dragon Fly.

LONG DUG   Greyhound.

"Ole Jan was up 'th rawd like a long dug".

LONG SLEEVE HAT   Top hat.

LONG SLEEVE CLOCK   Grandfather clock.

LONG TAILED RABBIT   Pheasant.

This expression is used by someone who is out shooting rabbits, but shoots a pheasant, would say to the Police, *"I'm sorry yer 'onner but I thought 'twas a Long Tailed Rabbit"*.

LOUSTERIN'   Hard work.
"Varmer be out all day Lousterin', Daychin' 'n a Ditchin'".

LURRAPIN'   Beating, hard smacking.
"If that cheal dawnt behaive, I'll give 'n sich a Lurrapin'".

MAID, MAID'N   Young girl (teenage).
Baby girl is known as a cheal. Some people refer to baby boys or girls as *'Cheal'*.

MAUNDERIN   Muttering, grumbling.
"'Th gurt vule, 'ee's always maunderin' to 'eez'el".

MAY BLOOTH   Hawthorn.

MAZZARDS, MAZZERDS   Damsons.

MEZEL   Myself.
"If you ask me, I kin tell 'ee I'd keep 'n to mezel".

MITCHIN   To play truant.

"Uz would mitch from school now and again, that was until the attendance officer caught up with 'ee".

MIZMAIZED   Confused. See also *'Flummoxed'.*

MOMMET   Scarecrow.

"Look at 'ee, 'ee looks a proper Mommet".

MOOT   Tree stump.

"Take this yer Vizgie 'n dig out thikky moot, will 'ee?".

MOOWAY, MOWHAY   Rick yard.

Stooks of corn would be stacked into ricks and stored in a Rick yard.

MORT, MORT'L - (1902)   A lot, large.

"Caw 'twas a mort'l size I tell 'ee me boody, I eb'm zin nort like it".

MOUTH SPAICH   Dialect.

"I tell 'ee buye, 'th ole Deb'm Dialect be 'th only mouth spaich to spaik".

MUMCHANCE   Mute, silent.

There are certain times when I wished certain people was a bit Mumchance.

MUMP AIDED   Silly.

You will sometimes hear the expression *'Addle Aided'* (slow witted).

MUTY ARTED   Soft hearted, easily upset.

"'Er be jist Muty Arted really, 'er id'n zo braave".

MUZCRAWL, MUSCRAW   Caterpillar.

NACK Knock.

This word would be heard in the sentence as a greeting.
"Ow be Nackin' Vore?". (How are you getting on?).

NAP The top of, horizon.

"'Ee's pon tap, nap 'o thikky ill (hill)".

NATLINS Intestines.

"Tiz no use drinkin' too much cuz' twill maake yer Natlins 'n Kidly's all Back Ze Vore".

NAW TIZ Know it is.

NIDDICK Hollow in the back of the neck.

NIMPINGANG Again a very old word for a Whitlow.

NITCH Notch. Large bundle of reed or straw.

"This yer 'ood eve got a Nitch in 'n".

NITTALS Hazel trees, bushes.

NORNNY This is an old Devon word for Northanhay (Exeter).

NORT, KNAW NORT Nothing. Know nothing.

"Get out 'ee's nort but a naw nort".

NUBBIES A yeast bun flavoured with saffron.

ON UPON What are you doing?

"What be on upon?".

OOD Wood.

There's nort better than turnin' a nice bit 'o 'ood on thikky lathe.

OOD-ALL This is an old Deb'm word for a woodpecker.

ODDS Difference.
"Dawnt maake no odds 't me buye".

OOZLE Whistle, throat.
"Come on me boody tiz time to wet yer oozle". (Have a drink).

ORNYWINK Lapwing.

ORT Something.
"Look at the size 'o thikky grub, tiz ort or nort". (Something and nothing).

ORT'S Odds, scraps.
"Uz 'ed better give thikky orts to 'th ole dug".

OSS Horse.
I don't like riding horses, I never can find the brakes.

O'T Of it.
"I dawnt think nort o' t".Pronounced *'Aw it'*.

OW DO 'EE DO How do you do.
Uz ask that sort 'o thing in Deb'm 'cuz uz be nice like that.

PAIKSIN', PAIKSIN' ABOUT Messing about.
"Do 'ee stop paiksin about?".

PASSON Parson.

PAWCHED (Poached).
A field all cut up by stock, making it *stoggy-stogged*. (See zugs).

26

PELLUM   Dust.

"Dawnt 'ee go up 'n thikky tallet, cuz you'll kick up all 'th pellum 'n 'twill maake a master mess".

PIXIE FLAX   Cotton grass.

PIXIE LAID, PISKY LAID   Led astray by the pixies.

If someone drinks too much and gets *'shamfered'* (drunk) and their feet go backwards when they want to go forward, they are accused of being *'pixie laid'*.

PLANCIN', PLANCHEEN   Planking, floorboards.

I have had to polish many Planchin's, that why I suffer with House Maids Knee!

POOK   Haycock.

A pile of hay after it has been *'Tedded'* (turned), which is collected and made into a *'Rick'*.

PON'TAP   On top of.
"Tiz Pon'tap thikky table". (It is on top of the table).

POPPLES   Pebbles.
You will often see this word in a place name, i.e. Newton Poppleford.

POSSIT   A drink of hot milk and mixed with ale to curdle.

QUAAZY, QUEEZY   Unwell.
"Poor cheal be terrible quaazy 'n looks like a tawd (toad) 'n a bucket".

QUAIL (1900)   Give up.
i.e. Grass left in the sun, becomes scorched and will soon get *'Quailed Up'*.

QUILLAWAY (1879)
A dialect word used a lot in the Plymouth area for a stye in the eye.

RAIMID   Stretched.

RAMES, RAYMES   Frame, skeleton.
"Will 'ee clean up they ole rames, me boody?.

RAMSHAKLED   Rickety.
"Do 'ee call 't mind ole ramshakled bike? 'Eed vauch 'n like a maize thing".

REZZEVOY   Reservoir.
"I tell 'ee me boody, ole rezzevoy eb'm got nort 'een 'n".

RIGMAROLE
A lot of talk or fuss, not understood too clearly, i.e. complex rules would be said to be an ole *'rigmarole'*.

RIMLETS   Remnants.

"Do 'ee pick up all they rimlets, cheal, tiz like a jumble sale yer".

RUMMIDGE, RUMMIGE   Rubbish, junk, nonsence.

"Jist git rid 'o this yer Rummage, will 'ee".

SCAT   Throw, cast, rain.

It is sometimes said *"A scat or scad 'o rain"*.
You would scat something away (throw). If you broke something into
shards, it could be said *"You scat 'n abroad"*.

SCUMMER   Muddle, mess, confusion.

"Did 'ee zee that meetin' 'twas a proper scummer".

SHIPPIN'   Shipon, Milking shed.

SHORDS, SHERDS,
SHARDS, SHEVVERS   Small pieces of broken pottery.

SKITTERS   Diarrhoea. No comment!

SKRIDDICK, SCRIDDICK   Bits and pieces.

SKRITCH   Screech, cry, scream.

"Listen 't they chillern maakin' thikky ole skritch".

SKRITCH OWL   Tawny Owl.

SLAMMICK, SLUMMICK, SLOMMICK   Untidy, sluggish.

"Did 'ee zee 'ee slummickin' about?".
It could well have been spelt without the 'c'.

SMITCH   Smoke. i.e. A fire, oil lamp, etc.

A frying pan is known as a *'Smitcher'*.

SPUDDLE	Potter about.

SPUDLEE	To busy one's self.
SQUAAL	Squeal.

"Caw will 'ee listen to that 'vear" sqaalin'".

SQUAB	Young pigeon.

There's nort better 'n a nice Squab Pie.

STOGGED, STUGGED	Bogged, unable to move, stoggy.

TALLET	Loft, Top shelf of a barn.

I expect most of 'ee eve bin up in 'th ole tallet of a barn, 'n made the pellum fall?.

TAW'D, TAWED	Toad.

This can be used in a reply to a greeting.
"Ow be nackin' vore?". "Oh I be like a Taw'd 'n a bucket". (Don't know which way to turn).

TAY	Tea.

Years ago it used to be spelt *'Tee'* and pronounced *'Tay'*.
See I told 'ee uz talk proper.

TEDDIES	Potatoes.

There's nort as good as a gurt teddy caake, twill line yer ribs.

THIKKY	This, that, the, those.

THRAIPIN'	Sort out, shake up.

"If you dawnt look out maid, I'll give 'ee one hang 'o a thraipin'".

THURDLE GUTTED   Thin, starved.

If you eat plenty of *'Teddy Cake'* you won't suffer with this problem.

TIBBY LAMBS   Baby Lambs.

TIFFLES, TIFFLIN'S   Bits of cotton, lint.

"Yer, yer cords be vull 'o tifflin's, get yerzel' yer   'n yer what I be tellin' to 'ee".

TIZZICK   Sick, unwell.

"What's a matter Maister, you baint lookin' very viddy?". "No buye I be veelin' proper tizzicky".

TRAADE   Trade.

Usually referred to food or a product. *"Whats this ole traade?".*

TRAIPSIN', TRAIPS   Walking, walk.

Uz likes to go traipsin' about Dartmoor at the weekend.

TRIVIT

Three legged stand for putting a kettle on next to an open 'arth.

TWADD'N   It wasn't.

"Twadd'n no good".

UNDERD, UNDURD   One hundred.

UZ   Us, we.

UZ-BE   We are.

UZ BETTER WAY   We had better.

UZ-EVE   We have.

UZ'L   We will.

UZ IZ   We are.

How to use this in a sentence? Simple, try this:

"Uz be gwain to, cuz uz be aidin' fer trouble, cuz uz eve done it once 'n uz'l do it again, uz ad better way, any how!".

VAUCHIN'   Move fast.

"That cheal be vauchin' 'th ole bike like a maizeound'". *(Mad dog)*.

VEAR   Piglets, sucking pig.

VEESH   Fish.

I love to go fishing with me buye, trouble is I usually end up with a 'Saltash Rig'. (Wet ass and no fish). (A Plymouth saying).

VEXED

I have come across two meanings to this. Bad tempered. Sorry.

VIGGY PUDDIN'   Fig pudding.

A good rib tickler.

VITTY, VIDDY   Well, alright, correct.

"Owe be nackin' vore?".
"Oh I be purt viddy me boody".

VIZGIE

A double bladded digging tool, which has one horizontal blade and one
verticle blade. Also sometimes called a *'Two Bill'*.

VURRINER   Foreigner.

This relates to anyone who is not born and bred from your village, town, etc.
Also another name here in Ashburton is *'A Blaw 'een"*. (A blow in).
I believe that there is a 20 year apprenticeship to be served before you are
accepted as a local in Devon.

VUST, VURST   First.

"Vust 'een, vust zerved".

VUTTY, VULTY   Filthy.

"They chillern eve bin traipsin' dro thikky yard 'n be proper vutty".

VUZKITE   Kestrel.

VUZZ   Furze, gorse.

Vuzz bush.

WANT   Mole.

This is a very old dialect word for a mole, and a mole hill was known as a *'Want Nap'*.

WESKIT   Waistcoat.

You can always tell a gentleman by the cut of his *'Weskit'*.

WHERT, WORTS, URTS   Whortleberry.

Also another name for this is *'Wertle Bertles'*, I sometimes tell visitors about *'Urts'*, but tell them that if they do go to get some on Dartmoor, they will have to purchase a *Vurn Ticket!*

WHIPS 'N WHILE   Occasionally, now and again.

"U'zl eve 't zee 'n every whips 'n while, else 'ee may end up 'zam zawed'"

WINNARD   Heron.

"Look to 'th length 'o 'ee, 'tiz like a winnard".

WISH 'EE WELL   Wish you well.

An expression often heard in *Deb'm*.

WISS, WUSS   Worse.

YAFFERS, YAWS   Heifers and Ewes.

YAPPIN'   Talking.

I expect you know somebody who enjoys a good *yap?*

YEMMERS, YEMMORS   Embers, hot ashes.

"Yer 'tiz time fer 'ee 't clean out 'th ole yemmers 'n thikky open arth, me boody".

YER

Year, hear, ear, here.

A good explanation of the word;

"Yer git yer zel yer 'n yer what you kin yer cuz yer 'n's better 'n mine"

YORKS

Leather or Binder Twine tied just below the knees to help keep the bottom of the trousers out of the mud and such like.

YU'M

You are.

"Yu'm a gurt gawk, dawnt 'ee naw nort?". Also *'Yu be'* will be used.

ZACKLY

Exactly.

"'Tiz zackly ez uz zaid twude be".

ZAMZOIY, ZAMZAWED

Sour.

Tea that has been left for some time and has got a bit stale could be said to be *Zamzawed*. (*Zamzodden* is something spoiled).

ZEX

No it's not what you think it is. It stands for six.

i.e.   1 - *Wan;*
3 - *Dree;*
4 - *Vower;*
5 - *Vive;*
6 - *Zex;*
7 - *Zeb'm;*
11 - *Leb'm;*   and so on.

ZINDAY SKULE TRAIT

Sunday School Treat. I can remember my Sunday School treat was always to go to Paignton Beach with two sisters known in Ashburton as the 'Miss Butlers', who ran the Sunday School. This took place once a year, every year.

ZINDY BOOTS   Sunday boots.

Work boots had hobs on the sole, but Sunday boots had no hobs (so I've been told)!

ZINDY CLAWS   Sunday clothes.

These were clothes kept for special events like Harvest Festival etc.

ZOUR-ZAB   Bad tempered.

A lovely sounding Devon word, why not try it?

ZUENT, SUENT   Smooth.

"This yer traade, do go down maister zuent".

ZUGS   Bogs. Soft ground (see *stogged*).

ZUMMAT, ZUMMIT   Something.

ZWANT, SWANT   Soft, pliable.

Not to be confused with *'Zuent'*.

"GWAIN ABROAD?" NO, GWAIN MAIZE!

My first visit to France. When the Twinning Association of Ashburton celebrated its 10th anniversary with Cleder they suggested that I, as Portreeve, should go along. Well, I was not too certain, especially as I feel sick just filling a bath. Anyway I went and this is what came out of it.

"If you'm gwain to France, you have to git yourzelf a passport" said the missus. "What do'ee mean a passport"? I says, "Oh 'tiz a little ole book that you puts yer photo 'een 'n writes, who you be 'n where abouts you comes from". "What the hang fer" I say's "I knaws who I be and where I comes from". Well 'eys you might maister but ole thikky French dawnt"! "Well 'tiz nort to do with they", I say's. "Well you got to have one and that's that".

Next 'er said "Now you got to go 'n git youzelf some money", "What fer" I say's, "I already got some". "That i'dn no gude yer maize vule". "Why not"? I say's "tev bin good enough fer hunderds 'o yer's so far". "No", said the missus, "Tev got to be French money". Well by this time I was beginning to wish I'd never 'o said I would go.

Anyhow, off I goes to the ole bank and I say's to the maid behind the fence, "I'd like zome money to go to France with, if you please". "Certainly zur, would 'ee like francs"? "MY GURD NO", I say's, "let 'ee git 'ee's awn. I got enough problems lookin' avter me'zelf"! Well that made the ole maid behind the fence laaf, though I still i'dn quite sure why. Anyhows out I comes with me money.

"Right" say's the missus with a termined look on 'er faace, "off you goes now 'n git yer hair cut". "WHAAT" I said, "I only had it cut 'bout dree weeks agone". "You git it cut" 'er say's, 'n if 'er says get it cut, you get it cut!

Next day uz was up braave 'n early, cases packed 'n on our way to Plymouth. Caw twas a master big boat they called 'n a Furry, 'n I was most amazed how idle zome volks be. Do 'ee knaw, zome of em even had to drive their cars on ole thikky boat, cus they was too idle to walk on 'n.

I noticed on this yer boat that they had a bar, so I say's to the missus how I thought twas about time uz had ourselves a drink! So uz sits down at this yer bar 'n avter about dree 't vower pints I started to notice how the zea was tryin' to over taake the ole boat, then twude try to go back to the plaace where it just come from. Next, twude decide to try 'n git on top of 'n, then next time twude try 'n duck under 'n. Well, I kin tell 'ee that was 'nough fer me! 'N all at once me stummick decided 'eed try 'n do the saame, one minute twas down at me ankles 'n the next minute twas tryin' to come out droo the top 'o me haad. CAW MY DEAR ZAW, I thought I was gwain turn inzides out. That's the trouble when you try's to drink Foreign Scrumpy 'zee, tid'n no gude fer 'ee.

Anyhow all at once uz wuz there, Frenchland, uz soon parked up the 'ole boat 'n on our way out, when all at once some blawk with a station masters hat on say's "ev'e 'ee anythin' to declare zur"? "Only that I had me hair cut yesterday maister", "no", 'ee say's "ev 'ee got ort in yer cases"? Well what a maaze question I thought to mezelf, as if I'd bring 'n empty suitcase all the way to Frenchland fer nort! "Course I 'eve" I say's, so the next thing 'ee does is opens up the cases 'n starts having a good ferrit round to see what 'ee could vind. Then 'ee gits out a bit 'o chalk 'n starts to draw all over me case. "Yer" I say's, "if you want to do some drawin' you git yourzelf a pen 'n a bit 'o paper 'n a proper manner.

Well uz evenually gits passed ole station maister, and ketches sight of the French volks. Well you never will guess what happen' next. A French blawk 'bout dree furlongs high, with hands like sledge hammers, puts both 'ee's gurt hands on me shoulders 'n starts to kiss me; I would'n mind but 'ee even closed 'ees eyes. Well that done it fer me, now I was completely confussed, 'n on me way back to ole thikky boat. The missus said "Where be gwain"? "'ome I say's. I 'kin tell 'ee now that the next time somebody say's to me 'I'm gwain abroad fer 'n holiday', I shill tell 'n straight, "You take my advice maister 'n stay 'ome yer, cuz I dawnt knaw 'bout gwain abroad my boodie, you'm more likely to end up GWAIN MAAZE".

————

AND FINALLY

A farmer goes to the doctors with terrible stomach ache. After the doctor gives him a good check over the following conversation takes place:

Doctor: "Well Jan, I can't see anything wrong with you".

Jan: "But 'onest zur, the pain be master bad".

Doctor: "Well I don't understand it, oh just a minute, are you regular? Do you go regularly?

Jan: "Yes zur, I goes 7.30am every mornin' reglur es clockwork, niver missed".

Doctor: "Well there's no problem there then".

Jan: "That's what you think me boody, zee I dawnt get up 'till 8.30am"